Film & Television Scenes For Teens & Kids
By
Alan Dysert

All rights reserved. Printed in the United States of America. This book, and any part of it, may not be used or reproduced in any manner whatsoever without written permission.

This is a work of fiction. Names, characters, businesses, places, events, and incidents are either the products of the author's imagination or used in a fictitious manner.

ISBN: 978-0-578-50648-7

First Edition: May 2019

Copyright 2019 by Alan Dysert

I would like to dedicate this book to my wife, Michele, who has saved my life more than once. Without her positivity and love, I would not be here today.

Notes from the Author

I never planned to write a collection of scenes.

One day I was organizing the scenes I had written for kids and teens over my many years of teaching the craft to young actors and I realized there were well over 50 scenes that I had written for this purpose.

I wrote these scenes over the years because it is very difficult to find scenes for kids and teens that help train young actors to work in front of a camera.

I decided there would be other teachers and young actors that would like to have a collection of original scenes that were written specifically for "Acting for the Camera" training.

I hope this collection of scenes will help many young actors in their journeys to become great actors in film and television.

Break a leg!

Alan

Quick Tips for Believable Acting

After teaching kids and teens for over 25 years, I have come up with what I call "Quick Tips for Believable Acting." This will give you a good start. Remember that acting is a craft and it takes time and work to make a scene believable. Acting is not just about memorizing lines. Memorization is just part of what actors do. If you work on the scene properly, the memorization will take care of itself.

1. LISTENING. Listening is the most important skill of an actor. Listening means taking it all in. You must not only listen to the words. You need to hear all sounds and watch the body language of the other actor or actors. Everything affects your response to what they say or do, just like in real life.

2. LISTEN AND REACT. This is what humans do. We listen to what the other person says and we react to it. This means that the other person's words are just as important to you as your own words.

3. EYE CONTACT IS THE KEY TO CONNECTING WITH THE OTHER ACTOR. If you are not connecting with the other actor, the audience will not feel anything. If you really connect with the other actor, everyone will feel it.

4. IF YOU DO NOT FEEL IT, NO ONE ELSE WILL.

5. NEVER GET CAUGHT ACTING. If we can tell you're acting, we won't believe what you're saying. It will be just two actors reciting lines. You need to work the dialogue until it feels like real people talking about real things.

6. HAVE A REAL CONVERSATION. Your scene has to be a real conversation with the other actor.

7. KNOW WHAT YOUR CHARACTER REALLY WANTS IN THE SCENE. Our wants and needs are what drives us as humans all day, every day. This "want" will drive you through the scene.

8. KNOW THE OTHER ACTOR'S LINES AS WELL AS YOUR OWN. This will help you understand where the other character is coming from and what their wants and needs are in the scene. This is also the best way to understand what the writer is trying to communicate. You also need to know

when the other actor's line is complete. This is the only way you will know when to react.

9. FIND THE CONFLICT IN THE SCENE. Generally you will find that your character wants something totally different than the other character. This is what creates the conflict. You will find conflict in almost all dramatic and comedic scenes.

10. MAKE SURE YOUR BODY LANGUAGE MATCHES THE EMOTIONAL STATE OF YOUR CHARACTER. For example, you don't want your body to be relaxed when you have aggressive dialogue or when your character is afraid. As another example, you don't want to be fidgety when your character is supposed to be confident. Don't start the scene until your body and mind are connected.

11. SLOW DOWN. A scene is not a race. Make the words mean something. Savor the dialogue. You will know if the pace of a scene should be fast. Give yourself time to think, and then react.

12. LEARN TO STAND STILL. You want close-ups and you don't want your head to be moving all across the frame. This doesn't mean be stiff - just don't move your base. Pretend you are poured in concrete from the waist down. You can still move your arms and be natural from the waist up without messing up the shot.

13. MAKE SMALL MOVEMENTS. The camera exaggerates all movement. If you are going to look away or turn a little, make the movement smaller than you would in real life.

14. STAY IN PRESENT TIME. You should be looking at the other actor when they are talking, not looking at your lines or thinking about your next line (if the scene is not memorized yet). You should also be looking at the other actor when you are speaking (unless your character has a reason to look away). If you are looking at your lines or thinking about your next line when the other actor is speaking, you are in the FUTURE and your scene partner is in the PRESENT. You must both be in the PRESENT. Listen to the other actor's words like you would in a real conversation and then respond. Don't be in a hurry to respond. Give your brain time to think about what they just said before you respond.

15. HAVE FUN. This is the most important tip of all.

TABLE OF CONTENTS

Scenes for Teens - Dramatic

A Christmas Crime	15
Guilt	18
Left Alone	20
Fake Friend	22
Bad New Boyfriend	24
Get it Together, Girl	26
Just a Walk?	28
Insider Traders in the Making	30
Mystery of Mary	32
He is Trouble	34
Bad Choices	36
Anything Goes Scene 1	38
Anything Goes Scene 2	39

Scenes for Teens – Dramatic/Comedic

Anything Goes Scene 3	43
Anything Goes Scene 4	44
Hospitalphobia	45
Facing Fears	47
Bungee Buddies	50

Scenes for Teens – Comedic

Accidental Shoplifter	55
Aliens Write Great Term Papers	57
Copy Hat	59
Roses for Boys	61
Too Tight Jeans	63
Wishful Thinking (Girl Version)	65
Wishful Thinking (Boy Version)	67
What is Depression?	69
Boy Crazy	71
Francois from France	73
Give a Friend Credit?	76
Your Therapy Isn't Working	78

Scenes for Kids or Teens – Dramatic

Standing Up to the Bully	83
Run!	85

Scenes for Kids or Teens – Dramatic/Comedic

Student Shrink	89
County Fair Crisis	92
Fish Tank Terror	94
Sugar Isn't Your Friend	96
Time Machine	98
What's in Your Hand?	100

Scenes for Kids or Teens – Comedic

Favorite Sneakers	105
Tiny House	107
Weird Cousin Frank	109
Dog Treats Aren't for Humans	111
Goin' Vegetarian	113
I Hate Math	115
Motorcycles Need Keys	116
Don't Feed This Dog	118
Happy Mom?	120
Big Day at the Buffet	122
Gotta Get Rich	124
Silver Linings	126
Here, Kitty Kitty	128

Scenes for Kids – Dramatic/Comedic

Dogs Hate Me	131
No Cats	133

SCENES FOR TEENS - DRAMATIC

A CHRISTMAS CRIME

INT. POLICE STATION – DAY

Teen boys or girls.

          CHARACTER 1
I can't believe you stole that DVD.

          CHARACTER 2
It wasn't for me. You said you wanted it. I got it for you.

          CHARACTER 1
I want a lot of things, but that doesn't mean that I want you to steal 'em for me. If I told you I wanted a Corvette, would you steal that too?

          CHARACTER 2
Oh, come on. It was one DVD. They have thousands.

          CHARACTER 1
Well, look where it got us. My parents are gonna kill me.

          CHARACTER 2
You don't have anything to worry about. You didn't do anything. What are you worried about? I'm the one that's gonna catch all the grief.

          CHARACTER 1
I was dragged out of Walmart by the police and you tell me I'm not in trouble. I saw five people that I know when we were put in the squad car, including one of my teachers. It could be on the news tonight or in the paper tomorrow. If my grandma sees it, Christmas will be the biggest disaster of my life.

          CHARACTER 2
I'll straighten it out.

          CHARACTER 1
How are you gonna straighten it out? You'll be in jail. My best friend is going to be in jail.

CHARACTER 2
I won't be in jail. They don't put people in jail for somethin' little like picking up a DVD.

CHARACTER 1
Yes, they do. You think they're gonna give you the key to the city?

CHARACTER 2
This is the thanks I get for trying to get you your favorite movie for Christmas?

CHARACTER 1
I'm not so sure that's the idea behind Christmas. Stealing neat things for all your friends and family.

CHARACTER 2
Hey, buzz off. Easy for you to say. I don't have tons of money like you. You can buy anything you want for anyone you want. I get tired of having to give everyone junky stuff for Christmas. So why don't you just leave and forget about me?

CHARACTER 1
Well, unfortunately I'm in for questioning. So I can't leave even if I want to. My parents are gonna kill me. If you were going to steal, at least you could have done it right.

CHARACTER 2
Like you know anything about it.

CHARACTER 1
At least I'd be smart enough not to get caught.

CHARACTER 2
Like you're Mr. Big Time Criminal.

CHARACTER 1
No, and I don't wanna be. So after I get out of here, just leave me out of your next heist.

CHARACTER 2
I'll just leave you out of my life. How's that? I don't need you anyway, Mr./Ms. Perfect.

CHARACTER 1
I'm sorry. I don't mean I never want to see you again. I just wish we weren't here...and I wish I didn't have to call my parents and tell them I'm at the jail.

CHARACTER 2
Well, you don't get everything you wish for. Trust me...I know.

GUILT

EXT. NEIGHBORHOOD - DAY

Two teens (girls or boys) are walking in their neighborhood.

                    CHARACTER 1
          I hate guilt.

                    CHARACTER 2
          Where did that come from?

                    CHARACTER 1
          I just told my mom we had a big
          assignment that we have to work on
          for school so I couldn't hang out
          with her this evening.

                    CHARACTER 2
          I tell my mom stuff like that all
          the time.

                    CHARACTER 1
          I know, but your mom isn't really,
          really sick either.

                    CHARACTER 2
          How's she doing anyway?

                    CHARACTER 1
          Not good. She got some really bad
          test results.

                    CHARACTER 2
          Sorry.

                    CHARACTER 1
          I just don't know what to say to
          her. It's really sad.

                    CHARACTER 2
          Does she talk about it?

                    CHARACTER 1
          No. That's the thing - she doesn't
          tell me much - and I'm afraid to
          ask.

                    CHARACTER 2
          Is she gonna get better?

CHARACTER 1
I don't think so.

CHARACTER 2
I don't know what to say.

CHARACTER 1
There's nothing to say.

CHARACTER 2
How's your dad handling it?

CHARACTER 1
He's working all the time trying to pay for all the extra bills that the insurance doesn't pay.

CHARACTER 2
How much is it?

CHARACTER 1
I heard them talking when they didn't know I could hear them. Dad said it was up to over $100,000 now.

CHARACTER 2
Maybe you better go hang out with your mother.

CHARACTER 1
What do I tell her?

CHARACTER 2
Tell her you want to talk about whatever she wants to talk about.

CHARACTER 1
You're right. See ya tomorrow.

CHARACTER 2
Good luck.

LEFT ALONE

INT. SCHOOL HALLWAY - DAY

Teen boys or girls.

          CHARACTER 1
Did I do something wrong?

          CHARACTER 2
What do you mean?

          CHARACTER 1
You have been acting weird all morning.

          CHARACTER 2
I have not. You're nuts!

          CHARACTER 1
You have not said more than ten words to me.

          CHARACTER 2
Maybe I don't have anything to say.

          CHARACTER 1
That's funny.

          CHARACTER 2
What do you mean by that?

          CHARACTER 1
I mean - you usually never stop talking. You're like a talking machine.

          CHARACTER 2
I didn't know my talking bothered you so much. Guess I will just stop talking completely.

          CHARACTER 1
Is this all because I am going to a different school next year?

          CHARACTER 2
Maybe. Why are you leaving me here by myself?

                    CHARACTER 1
It's not my fault. My parents
bought a new house on the other
side of town.

                    CHARACTER 2
But now you'll have a new best
friend at your new school - and I'm
gonna be left alone with all these
weirdos.

FAKE FRIEND

EXT. DRIVEWAY OF SARA'S HOUSE - DAY

Teen girls.

> MAKENNA
> What is that?

> SARA
> What is what?

> MAKENNA
> What you're wearing. You are not wearing that to go to Beverly Hills!

> SARA
> Why not?

> MAKENNA
> Because it's gross. Really gross.

> SARA
> Who says you are the fashion goddess of Riverside, California?

> MAKENNA
> Because I can tell the difference between "good" and "Goodwill."

> SARA
> I am not going with you to Beverly Hills. Every time I try to experiment with my wardrobe, you put me down. You are the most opinionated person I have ever met.

> MAKENNA
> I am opinionated? Just because I don't want you to embarrass both of us in a town where style is everything.

> SARA
> Anyone can buy clothes off the rack at the stores you shop at. It takes no talent at all. You don't have a creative bone in your body.

> MAKENNA
> Is that right?

SARA
That is most definitely right.

MAKENNA
Well, the fact is that I am the one driving - and if you want to go with me - you are going to have to listen to some advice on what not to wear. And that rag is definitely not riding in my car.

SARA
The truth of the matter is that I don't really want to be seen riding in that ridiculous car of yours anyway. It is way too obvious.

MAKENNA
What is that supposed to mean?

SARA
Your car screams out "I am so insecure with myself that I have to drive this car."

MAKENNA
You wish you had my car.

SARA
I wish I had a different friend. That is what I wish.

Sara walks out.

MAKENNA
(screaming)
Good luck. I hope you meet somebody you like better at Goodwill.

BAD NEW BOYFRIEND

INT. COFFEE HOUSE - DAY

Teen girls.

              HOLLY
Thanks for meeting me.

              HANNAH
No problem. But I have to meet Reed in like 20 minutes.

              HOLLY
Ok. This won't take long.

              HANNAH
So what's so important?

              HOLLY
We have been friends since second grade and I hope we will still be friends when we are 50.

              HANNAH
I feel a heavy conversation coming on. You are being kinda cheesy overdramatic.

              HOLLY
I'm sorry, but I see you heading in a direction that's really dangerous.

              HANNAH
Oh let me guess - this has to do with Reed.

              HOLLY
As a matter of fact it does. He is trouble...and has been for years.

              HANNAH
Well, how about we just leave Reed out of any conversation we have.

              HOLLY
I can't leave Reed out of the conversation because I'm worried about you.

HANNAH
I think you're just jealous because you don't have anybody special in your life.

HOLLY
No, I don't have a boyfriend but this has nothing to do with that.

HANNAH
Right.

HOLLY
You are getting C's and D's in your classes now. You used to get all A's. You lie to your parents all the time and ask us to cover for you.

HANNAH
So what! School is stupid.

HOLLY
That sounds like something Reed would say - not you.

HANNAH
Reed sees school for what it is - a waste of time. We're writing music. We're gonna change the world.

HOLLY
So, you're a songwriter now? Good luck with that.

HANNAH
Good luck being a loser.

HOLLY
You dress like him...you act like him...and now you talk like him. Pretty sad that the Hannah I knew is dead.

HANNAH
This conversation is over.

GET IT TOGETHER, GIRL

INT. STARBUCKS - DAY

Teen girls.

Sara walks into Starbucks where she meets her friend, Shelby, most every Saturday afternoon. Shelby has just seen her ex-boyfriend, Matt, with a girl that he dumped her for over the summer - a girl she thought was going back to California when school started. She was just in town for the summer to be with her father. Shelby had hoped Matt would come crawling back after the summer, but it seems there has been a change of plans.

                SARA
What's wrong?

                SHELBY
I saw him.

                SARA
That's good, isn't it?

                SHELBY
No.

                SARA
Why not?

                SHELBY
Because he was with her.

                SARA
I thought she went back to California.

                SHELBY
Obviously not.

                SARA
What did he say?

                SHELBY
Nothing. He looked the other way and pretended that he didn't see me.

                SARA
I wish I would have been there. I would have punched him in the face. Her too.

                    SHELBY
          I don't know how to stop thinking
          about it. I just keep seeing them
          walking away holding hands.

                    SARA
          Snap out of it. You are stronger
          than that. You don't need him. He
          is obviously a jerk.

                    SHELBY
          You don't know.

                    SARA
          I know you can't keep doing this.
          Come on, let's go.

Sara pulls her out of the chair.

                    SHELBY
          Where are we going?

                    SARA
          To find a guy who knows a good
          woman when he's got one.

JUST A WALK?

INT. KITCHEN - DAY

Daughter/son (teen boy or girl) casually walks toward the back door.

          MOM
Where are you going?

          DAUGHTER/SON
For a walk.

          MOM
No you're not.

          DAUGHTER/SON
Why not?

          MOM
Because you're grounded.

          DAUGHTER/SON
And that means I can't even walk down the street to get some exercise?

          MOM
I know where you're going.

          DAUGHTER/SON
I said I was going for a walk.

          MOM
Ok. Then I'll go with you.

          DAUGHTER/SON
What?

          MOM
If you want to exercise so badly, you won't mind me walking with you.

          DAUGHTER/SON
Never mind.

          MOM
That's what I thought.

          DAUGHTER/SON
This is ridiculous.

MOM
Study. That will pass the time.

INSIDER TRADERS IN THE MAKING

EXT. SECRET MEETING PLACE IN THE NEIGHBORHOOD - NIGHT

Teen boy and girl.

          MAC
Ok, this is what I need from you. I need you to ask your dad how things are going with the company.

          AUBRIE
Why? I never ask him stuff like that.

          MAC
Well, that is about to change. You are about to be very interested.

          AUBRIE
Why?

          MAC
Because you want to follow in his footsteps.

          AUBRIE
That is not true. Whatever it is he does is boring.

          MAC
Your father is worth 300 million because he does something boring. And he isn't giving it to you. I read online that he just gave 10 million to State University.

          AUBRIE
What?

          MAC
How much did he give you?

Aubrie doesn't answer.

          MAC (CONT'D)
Exactly! And that is why we have to do what we are going to do.

          AUBRIE
We're going to steal money from my dad?

MAC
No, Goober! We are just going to make some money from information we get from him.

AUBRIE
What kind of information?

MAC
You just leave that to me. Your job is to start acting like you're interested. And ask a lot of questions - that I will feed you.

AUBRIE
And how will we make money from this?

MAC
Some people would call it "insider trading." But I have a way to get around that.

AUBRIE
That sounds illegal.

MAC
Only if someone figures it out. But they won't. Tell no one - and we leave no paper trail - no emails, no texts. You could end up a very rich young woman - and no one will ever have to know.

AUBRIE
Nobody will know?

MAC
Just me - and you.

MYSTERY OF MARY

LOCATION - ACTOR'S CHOICE

Teen boys or girls.

>CHARACTER 1
>How can everyone just let it go? Mary did not just vanish into thin air.

>CHARACTER 2
>The police said she was a runaway.

>CHARACTER 1
>Runaway? That is ridiculous! She had no reason to run away. From what was she running? She has great parents and she is the happiest friend we have.

>CHARACTER 2
>I don't know. Don't get mad at me. I didn't have anything to do with it. It's not our job. That's her parents' job...and the police.

>CHARACTER 1
>It's like the police know something - but are keeping it to themselves.

>CHARACTER 2
>So you think the police have her?

>CHARACTER 1
>I don't know...but I can feel it. Something is really wrong here. I think she is still here - in town. She did not run off to California or something stupid like that. She would have told us.

>CHARACTER 2
>You mean you think she was abducted?

>CHARACTER 1
>I don't know, but we have to do something because nothing is getting done. It's like they have given up already.

CHARACTER 2
Ok. What is our first step?

CHARACTER 1
I'm thinking.

CHARACTER 2
Well, you better think quick...because here come two policemen.

CHARACTER 1
Act normal and don't mention Mary.

HE IS TROUBLE

INT. STARBUCKS AT AN UPSCALE MALL - DAY

Teen girls.

Character 1 comes rushing in.

          CHARACTER 1
Sorry I'm late.

          CHARACTER 2
What happened?

          CHARACTER 1
I've been in the mall - but I ran into someone.

          CHARACTER 2
Someone?

          CHARACTER 1
Let's get our drinks.

          CHARACTER 2
You are not getting off that easy.

          CHARACTER 1
What?

          CHARACTER 2
I asked you who "someone" was - and you totally ignored me.

          CHARACTER 1
That's because it was no big deal.

          CHARACTER 2
It must be a pretty big deal since you won't tell me.

          CHARACTER 1
Ok. But don't make a big deal about it.

          CHARACTER 2
About what?

          CHARACTER 1
I was hanging out with Mark Jeffers.

                    CHARACTER 2
               (freaking out)
          You are in so much trouble!

                    CHARACTER 1
          This is exactly why I didn't tell
          you.

                    CHARACTER 2
          Your dad will kill him.

                    CHARACTER 1
          And that is why you are not going
          to tell anyone.

                    CHARACTER 2
          He is like 3 years older than you
          are. And he used to date your
          sister. Remember how that turned
          out?

                    CHARACTER 1
          I don't see what the big deal is.
          My dad is 5 years older than my
          mom.

                    CHARACTER 2
          That is totally different. They're
          old.

                    CHARACTER 1
          He says I'm very mature for my age.

                    CHARACTER 2
          He is "trouble." Everybody knows
          that.

                    CHARACTER 1
          They don't know him like I know
          him. He's just misunderstood.

                    CHARACTER 2
          I think I'm going to throw up right
          here in Starbucks.

BAD CHOICES

EXT. FRONT STEPS - DAY

Teen boys or girls.

Character 1 comes home to find Character 2 sitting on his/her front steps.

              CHARACTER 1
Hey, what are you doing here?

              CHARACTER 2
Lookin' for you.

              CHARACTER 1
Well, here I am. Why now?

              CHARACTER 2
What do you mean?

              CHARACTER 1
I dunno - you just kinda stopped coming around - or even talking to me or any of our friends.

              CHARACTER 2
I know.

              CHARACTER 1
So what's the deal?

              CHARACTER 2
The deal is that I'm so mixed up I can't even think straight.

              CHARACTER 1
What happened?

              CHARACTER 2
I think I finally realized that I dumped my friends that are "good people" for some other people that are not "good people" at all.

              CHARACTER 1
I could have told you that back when you first started hangin' out with them.

CHARACTER 2
I know. I just got tempted to be a little edgier than I was. I felt like I was the straightest person in the world.

CHARACTER 1
So what happened?

CHARACTER 2
They turned out to be way too edgy. I almost did some stuff I shouldn't do.

CHARACTER 1
Well, at least you were smart enough to get out before it was too late.

CHARACTER 2
I think I want to go back to who I was - or at least close to who I was. I will never be able to be exactly who I was.

CHARACTER 1
Welcome back. But maybe we'll be just a little edgier so you won't get bored.

CHARACTER 2
Ok. Sounds good.

ANYTHING GOES SCENE 1

Teen boys or girls.

Actors should create their own characters, location, and situation.

>   CHARACTER 1
> Can you believe that?
>
>   CHARACTER 2
> No.
>
>   CHARACTER 1
> What are we gonna do?
>
>   CHARACTER 2
> I'm thinking.
>
>   CHARACTER 1
> This is really big.
>
>   CHARACTER 2
> We can manage it.
>
>   CHARACTER 1
> Got any ideas?
>
>   CHARACTER 2
> Yes. But don't tell anyone.

ANYTHING GOES SCENE 2

Teen boys or girls.

Actors should create their own characters, location, and situation.

CHARACTER 1
What's with you?

CHARACTER 2
What?

CHARACTER 1
You know what.

CHARACTER 2
Don't think I do.

CHARACTER 1
You almost run away when you see me.

CHARACTER 2
That's stupid.

CHARACTER 1
You're acting stupid.

CHARACTER 2
You have no idea what's going on in my life.

CHARACTER 1
Maybe you should tell me then.

CHARACTER 2
I would if I thought it would make a difference.

CHARACTER 1
It's not good to drive all your friends away.

CHARACTER 2
I think most of them are already gone.

SCENES FOR TEENS - DRAMATIC/COMEDIC

ANYTHING GOES SCENE 3

Teen boys or girls.

Actors should create their own characters, location, and situation. Try to do this as a dramatic scene and then as a comedic scene.

           CHARACTER 1
Are we there?

           CHARACTER 2
I don't know. Maybe.

           CHARACTER 1
What is that?

           CHARACTER 2
Can't you tell?

           CHARACTER 1
Why can't you just tell me?

           CHARACTER 2
You know why.

           CHARACTER 1
Do you need me to get it?

           CHARACTER 2
Yes.

           CHARACTER 1
There. What do you think of that?

           CHARACTER 2
Oh, that's great.

           CHARACTER 1
You know, some days I wonder about you.

           CHARACTER 2
I never wonder about you. Here, take this.

           CHARACTER 1
What do you want me to do with this?

           CHARACTER 2
That's your problem now.

ANYTHING GOES SCENE 4

Teen boys or girls.

Actors should create their own characters, location, and situation. Try to do this first as a dramatic scene and then as a comedic scene.

          CHARACTER 1
What do you want?

          CHARACTER 2
I think you know.

          CHARACTER 1
I told you not to come back.

          CHARACTER 2
Under the circumstances, I couldn't do that.

          CHARACTER 1
I don't care about the circumstances. I don't want to talk to you.

          CHARACTER 2
Maybe you will change your mind when you see what I have to show you.

          CHARACTER 1
I doubt it.

          CHARACTER 2
I found this.

          CHARACTER 1
Where did you get that?

HOSPITALPHOBIA

INT. HOSPITAL - DAY

Three teen girls.

First try this scene as a comedic scene, then as a dramatic scene.

Shannon is lying in bed with an IV and other equipment attached to her.

Meghan and Bree stand at the door.

Shannon is napping.

> MEGHAN
> (whispering)
> Should we wake her up?

> BREE
> No. Let's leave.

Bree starts to go. Meghan stops her.

> MEGHAN
> We have to stay and talk to her. She's really sick.

> SHANNON
> I heard that.

> MEGHAN
> Sorry.

> BREE
> Yeah, sorry. We should go and let you rest.

> SHANNON
> No! Why would you leave?

> MEGHAN
> We're not leaving. Are we, Bree?

> BREE
> I'm sorry. Hospitals just kinda creep me out.

> SHANNON
> Me too...but I don't have a choice.

                    BREE
Guess not.

                    MEGHAN
We brought you some flowers.

                    BREE
And a dream catcher.

                    SHANNON
Thanks! You're the best.

                    MEGHAN
How are you feeling?

                    SHANNON
Pretty terrible.

                    BREE
What do you have?

                    SHANNON
They told my parents that it's some weird, rare blood disease. One in a hundred million people have it.

                    MEGHAN
Wow!

                    BREE
          (worried and naive)
Is it catching?

                    SHANNON
          (laughing)
No.

                    MEGHAN
If it were, do you think they would let us in here?

                    BREE
I just asked. Jeez.

                    MEGHAN
As you may remember...our friend, Bree, is a little bit of a hypochondriac.

FACING FEARS

INT. SCHOOL HALLWAY - MORNING

Teen boys or girls.

Try to make this a dramatic scene and then make it a comedic scene.

Alex and Taylor stand at their lockers.

          TAYLOR
I have some great news.

          ALEX
What?

          TAYLOR
You know how I told you my parents are taking me to Hawaii with them this summer?

          ALEX
Yes.

          TAYLOR
Well - I asked them if I could take a friend and they said I could.

          ALEX
And...

          TAYLOR
Guess who I want to take?

          ALEX
Who?

          TAYLOR
I want to take you, silly.

          ALEX
I can't go.

          TAYLOR
Why not?

          ALEX
Because...I won't be available.

TAYLOR
I didn't even tell you the dates of
the trip yet.

ALEX
I know but I'm going to have a
crazy summer.

TAYLOR
That is crazy! You just told me two
days ago that this summer is going
to be the most boring summer ever.
What could have changed so much in
two days?

ALEX
I'm going to get a job.

TAYLOR
You're not going to get a job.
There are no jobs.

ALEX
Ok...my parents won't let me. I
think it's a trust issue.

TAYLOR
Your parents are my parents' best
friends. There is no trust issue.
You are just making stuff up. There
is something else going on.

ALEX
Maybe I just don't want to go.

TAYLOR
Who doesn't want to go to
Hawaii...FOR FREE? All expenses
paid...WITH THEIR BEST FRIEND.

Alex says nothing.

TAYLOR (CONT'D)
Tell me the truth.

ALEX
(embarrassed)
I'm afraid to fly. Ok. There it is.
Are you happy?

TAYLOR
That's it?

ALEX

Yes.

TAYLOR

Why couldn't you just say that? Lots of people have a fear of flying.

ALEX

Because it's embarrassing. I'm supposed to be the fearless one. I want to go...but I just don't think I can get on the plane to get there.

TAYLOR

I'm your friend. We are going to get you over this little obstacle...or my name isn't Taylor Talbert. Ok?

ALEX

Ok.

BUNGEE BUDDIES

INT. TRAIN CAR - DAY

Two teens, boys or girls, sitting on a commuter train.

                    CHARACTER 1
This is going to be the greatest day of our lives.

                    CHARACTER 2
I hope so.

                    CHARACTER 1
What's with the negative tone?

                    CHARACTER 2
I'm starting to worry.

                    CHARACTER 1
Worry about what?

                    CHARACTER 2
That we are making a big mistake.

                    CHARACTER 1
How long have we been talking about doing this?

                    CHARACTER 2
A year I guess.

                    CHARACTER 1
So don't you think it is time to actually do it?

                    CHARACTER 2
I'm starting to think that maybe I never really wanted to do it. I was just caught up in your excitement.

                    CHARACTER 1
You are not going to blame this on me just because you are afraid.

                    CHARACTER 2
It just never seemed real before. But reality is sinking in now.

                    CHARACTER 1
"Fear is the Mind-Killer."

CHARACTER 2
What does that mean?

CHARACTER 1
It's a famous quote by a very wise man.

CHARACTER 2
And we lied to our parents. And we forged their signatures on the release form.

CHARACTER 1
Who's going to know?

CHARACTER 2
You said we are going to film it all - and do a huge social media blitz - and get a million hits on YouTube.

CHARACTER 1
And we will.

CHARACTER 2
So you don't think our parents will hear about it?

CHARACTER 1
My parents did a lot of crazy stuff when they were our age.

CHARACTER 2
Did they bungee jump from a 100 foot bridge?

CHARACTER 1
No. I don't even think anyone did bungee jumping way back then.

CHARACTER 2
Maybe there's a reason no one did it way back then.

CHARACTER 1
And what's the reason?

CHARACTER 2
Because it's STUPID!

SCENES FOR TEENS - COMEDIC

ACCIDENTAL SHOPLIFTER

INT. HALFWAY DOWN THE MALL - DAY

Two teen girls.

          CHARACTER 1
Oh no!

          CHARACTER 2
What?

          CHARACTER 1
I just found those earrings I tried on at Macy's in my coat pocket.

          CHARACTER 2
You stole them?

          CHARACTER 1
No, I didn't steal them. I guess you distracted me when you said to look at the cute guy.

          CHARACTER 2
Don't blame it on me.

          CHARACTER 1
I would never shoplift.

          CHARACTER 2
Well, you just did.

          CHARACTER 1
No, I didn't!

          CHARACTER 2
They will have you on the surveillance cameras in the store.

          CHARACTER 1
What?

          CHARACTER 2
They have cameras all over the store. They will probably be knocking on your door today.

          CHARACTER 1
They don't know who I am. That is ridiculous.

CHARACTER 2
They have facial recognition software. They can find anyone just from their face. Just like the FBI or the CIA.

CHARACTER 1
What should I do?

CHARACTER 2
Turn yourself into the police now and they'll go easier on you and give you a lighter sentence.

CHARACTER 1
I'm going back to Macy's and tell them what happened. They'll understand. Come on.

CHARACTER 2
No way!

CHARACTER 1
What?

CHARACTER 2
I can't be seen with you.

CHARACTER 1
You're gonna make me go by myself?

CHARACTER 2
Yes. I have my reputation to protect.

ALIENS WRITE GREAT TERM PAPERS

INT. SCHOOL - DAY

Three teen boys or girls.

Character 1 rushes into the school and runs up to two friends.

     CHARACTER 1
Ok - you aren't going to believe this.

     CHARACTERS 2 & 3
Probably won't.

     CHARACTER 1
I know I've been known to exaggerate a little at times - but I swear on my brother's life what I'm about to tell you is true.

     CHARACTER 2
You don't even like your brother.

     CHARACTER 3
You said you don't even think he is your brother.

     CHARACTER 1
Ok - bad choice of sacrifices. Then I swear on my new iPhone that what I am about to tell you is true.

     CHARACTER 2
Better...

     CHARACTER 3
But not impressive. Ok - what?

     CHARACTER 1
You know the paper we have due today?

     CHARACTER 2
Don't tell me - you forgot to do it.

     CHARACTER 1
No.

CHARACTER 3
Your dog ate it?

CHARACTER 1
No. I fell asleep last night when I was trying to get started. But when I woke up - it was all finished - printed - and ready to turn in. And it is an amazing paper!

CHARACTER 3
What are you saying?

CHARACTER 1
Here comes the hard to believe part. I had a dream that I had an alien tutor helping me with my paper. It must have really happened. Look at this paper! I could never write like that.

Characters 2 & 3 are shocked.

CHARACTER 2
No you couldn't.

COPY HAT

INT. PIZZA JOINT - NIGHT

Teen boys or girls.

          CHARACTER 1
That hat is awesome!!

          CHARACTER 2
Thanks. I love it!

          CHARACTER 1
It's a great image. Very cool.

          CHARACTER 2
I definitely think it says a lot about who I am.

          CHARACTER 1
Where did you get it?

          CHARACTER 2
I don't want to tell you.

          CHARACTER 1
Why not?

          CHARACTER 2
Honestly?

          CHARACTER 1
Yes.

          CHARACTER 2
Because every time I buy something that you like - you go out and buy the same thing.

          CHARACTER 1
No, I don't.

          CHARACTER 2
Yes, you do.

          CHARACTER 1
Like what?

          CHARACTER 2
My leather jacket, my new Nikes, my basketball jersey that says "Curry" on the back...

CHARACTER 1
Ok. So what. Who cares?

CHARACTER 2
I do. I don't want to run around with you looking like twins. You need to find your own image - not copy mine.

CHARACTER 1
Some friend you are.

ROSES FOR BOYS

INT. GIRLS LOCKER ROOM - DAY

Teen girls.

          ANNIE
Look - I have something I need to tell you.

          MARY
What?

          ANNIE
This is not easy to say - but as your friend - I feel it is my duty.

          MARY
Stop beating around the bush and tell me.

          ANNIE
Ok. You try too hard.

          MARY
What is that supposed to mean?

          ANNIE
For example - you like Michael Frost - so you sent him a dozen roses. Girls don't send boys roses. Especially not at our age.

          MARY
Who says?

          ANNIE
Trust me. Ask anyone in the world and they will tell you that will never work.

          MARY
Worked for me.

          ANNIE
What does that mean?

          MARY
He asked me if I want to go to a concert with him this weekend.

                    ANNIE
What?

                    MARY
And dinner.

                    ANNIE
What was the name of that flower
shop?

TOO TIGHT JEANS

INT. CHARACTER 1'S BEDROOM - NIGHT

Two teen girls.

          CHARACTER 1
I am telling you these new jeans fit me perfectly just two weeks ago.

          CHARACTER 2
Well, they definitely don't fit you now.

          CHARACTER 1
Thanks a lot.

          CHARACTER 2
Well, it's not like it's a secret. You can't even begin to button them.

          CHARACTER 1
What could have happened in just two weeks?

          CHARACTER 2
Probably the cruise you just went on with your parents.

          CHARACTER 1
I couldn't pack it on that fast.

          CHARACTER 2
My dad said he gained 20 pounds once on a cruise.

          CHARACTER 1
But look at your dad.

          CHARACTER 2
What's that supposed to mean?

          CHARACTER 1
Your dad is pretty porky. Don't compare me to your porky dad.

          CHARACTER 2
Hey, don't talk about my dad that way. He used to be an athlete.

CHARACTER 1
Well, he isn't now. What am I going to do?

CHARACTER 2
The fact is - you can't fasten your jeans - and you have nothing else to wear.

CHARACTER 1
Drive me home so I can change into something else.

CHARACTER 2
I can't drive you home.

CHARACTER 1
Why?

CHARACTER 2
I'll be an hour late for the party if I take you home.

CHARACTER 1
I can't go like this!

CHARACTER 2
There's an old pair of my brother's jeans in my trunk. You can wear those.

CHARACTER 1
You can't be serious!

CHARACTER 2
At least you would be able to button them. You might set a trend.

WISHFUL THINKING (GIRL VERSION)

INT. MALL - NIGHT

Two teen girls sit on a bench at the mall.

                    CHARACTER 1
Check it out. Be discreet. That gorgeous guy over there is looking at me and smiling.

                    CHARACTER 2
I don't see who you're talking about.

                    CHARACTER 1
Over there at 10:00. Don't be obvious.

                    CHARACTER 2
The one in the blue?

                    CHARACTER 1
No, not him, dummy. The gorgeous one in the red sweatshirt.

                    CHARACTER 2
Oh, wow! He has to be 18 if he's a day!

                    CHARACTER 1
You can say that again.

                    CHARACTER 2
Now he's pointing you out to his also very gorgeous friend. Maybe they want to double date?

                    CHARACTER 1
Give me a break. His friend would never be interested in you.

                    CHARACTER 2
What do you mean by that?

                    CHARACTER 1
He is way too cool for you.

                    CHARACTER 2
Oh, but the other guy isn't too cool for you?

CHARACTER 1
Obviously not. He just keeps looking at me and smiling.

CHARACTER 2
They're coming this way. Be cool.

CHARACTER 1
You be cool. He's already totally into how cool I am.

Both girls smile as the boys come closer. Then the boys walk right past them to two older teenage girls that have been standing behind our two girls.

CHARACTER 2
Were those girls standing there the whole time?

CHARACTER 1
I don't want to talk about it.

CHARACTER 2
I understand. You're too cool to talk about it.

CHARACTER 1
Shut up!

WISHFUL THINKING (BOY VERSION)

INT. MALL - NIGHT

Two friends (pre-teen or teen boys) sit on a bench at the mall.

                      CHARACTER 1
Check it out. Be discreet. That beautiful girl over there is looking at me and smiling.

                      CHARACTER 2
I don't see who you're talking about.

                      CHARACTER 1
Over there at 10:00. Don't be obvious.

                      CHARACTER 2
The one in the blue?

                      CHARACTER 1
No, not her, dummy. The gorgeous one in the pink sweatshirt.

                      CHARACTER 2
Oh, wow!

                      CHARACTER 1
You can say that again.

                      CHARACTER 2
Now she's pointing you out to her beautiful friend. Maybe they want to double date?

                      CHARACTER 1
Give me a break. Her friend would never be interested in you.

                      CHARACTER 2
What do you mean by that?

                      CHARACTER 1
She is way too cool for you.

                      CHARACTER 2
Oh, but the other girl isn't too cool for you?

                    CHARACTER 1
          Obviously not. She just keeps
          looking at me and smiling.

                    CHARACTER 2
          They're coming this way. Be cool.

                    CHARACTER 1
          You be cool. She's already totally
          into how cool I am.

Both boys smile as the girls come closer. Then the girls
walk right past them to two older teenage boys that have
been standing behind our two young guys.

                    CHARACTER 2
          Were those guys standing there the
          whole time?

                    CHARACTER 1
          I don't want to talk about it.

                    CHARACTER 2
          I understand. You're too cool to
          talk about it.

                    CHARACTER 1
          Shut up!

WHAT IS DEPRESSION?

INT. BEDROOM – DAY

Teen girls or boys.

Character 1's bedroom.

          CHARACTER 1
Can I ask you a question – confidentially?

          CHARACTER 2
Sure.

          CHARACTER 1
How does a person know if they're depressed?

          CHARACTER 2
I have no idea because I have never been depressed.

          CHARACTER 1
How do you know you've never been depressed?

          CHARACTER 2
What do you mean?

          CHARACTER 1
I mean – if you don't know what it feels like to be depressed – then how do you know you've never been depressed?

          CHARACTER 2
I think I would know if I were depressed.

          CHARACTER 1
How?

          CHARACTER 2
I just would.

          CHARACTER 1
Would what?

          CHARACTER 2
Know!

CHARACTER 1
Knowing suggests knowledge of the subject - but you have no knowledge - so it is possible that you are depressed all the time.

CHARACTER 2
That is ridiculous!

CHARACTER 1
Tell your psychiatrist that.

CHARACTER 2
I don't have a psychiatrist!

CHARACTER 1
Maybe you should consider it.

CHARACTER 2
You are driving me crazy!

CHARACTER 1
That is one of the first signs of depression.

CHARACTER 2
What is one of the first signs?

CHARACTER 1
Thinking you're going crazy.

BOY CRAZY

INT. CAR - NIGHT

Two teen girls are sitting in a car wearing hoodies.

          CHARACTER 1
Ok, why did you tell me to wear a hoodie?

          CHARACTER 2
You'll see.

          CHARACTER 1
I'll see what?

          CHARACTER 2
Quick. Scrunch down in the seat.

          CHARACTER 1
What?

          CHARACTER 2
GET DOWN!

          CHARACTER 1
Have you gone crazy?

          CHARACTER 2
Yes. Crazy in love.

          CHARACTER 1
I don't want to be a part of this. We are stalking.

          CHARACTER 2
HOODS UP!

          CHARACTER 1
I am not putting my hood up.

          CHARACTER 2
    (screaming)
If you don't put your hood up, I will have to put it up for you.

          CHARACTER 1
Ok. Ok. Whose house is that anyway?

          CHARACTER 2
Brandon Oliver.

CHARACTER 1
The new boy at school?

CHARACTER 2
That's the one. He is going to be mine - even if it kills me.

CHARACTER 1
He's only been at our school for 2 days. Give the guy a chance to settle in.

CHARACTER 2
I'm going to learn everything I can about him before any of the loser girls at our school get their hooks in him.

CHARACTER 1
How did you find out where he lives?

CHARACTER 2
My mom's in real estate. She helped me out?

CHARACTER 1
Your mom is in on this with you?

CHARACTER 2
Yep. I took a picture of him with my phone and showed it to her.

CHARACTER 1
And?

CHARACTER 2
She said "Go for it girl."

FRANCOIS FROM FRANCE

INT. SCHOOL HALLWAY - DAY

Teen girls.

Jada runs up to her friend, Caroline, who is putting her coat in her locker.

          JADA
Have you seen the new boy that just enrolled yesterday?

          CAROLINE
Have I seen him? His parents bought the house next to ours.

          JADA
You've got to be kidding.

          CAROLINE
Totally serious.

          JADA
Get out! Don't lie to me.

          CAROLINE
I can prove it.

Caroline pulls out her phone and shows Jada a picture she took of him from her bedroom window.

          CAROLINE (CONT'D)
He is pretty dreamy.

          JADA
Dreamy is not the word I was thinking of. I can't believe you took a picture of him.

          CAROLINE
I saw him take a picture of me first.

          JADA
I am going to move into your house.

          CAROLINE
And the coolest part...he is from France.

JADA
You're killing me!

CAROLINE
And who do you know that has taken four years of French?

JADA
Just my luck. I've been taking Spanish.

CAROLINE
Sorry.

JADA
Teach me some French. Quick!

CAROLINE
I can't just teach you French. It takes years.

JADA
Ok...then just teach me the cool accent.

CAROLINE
You're going to use a fake accent to talk to Francois?

JADA
His name is Francois? It sounds so cool coming out of your mouth.

CAROLINE
I know.

JADA
(makes a very bad attempt to say Francois and butchers his name)
Franzsoys?

CAROLINE
Forget it. Maybe you'll get lucky and a Spanish speaking boy will move in next to you.

JADA
But I want this particular French boy.

                    CAROLINE
          C'est dommage. (French for "too
          bad")

Caroline walks away.

                    JADA
             (yelling after her)
          Some friend you are!

GIVE A FRIEND CREDIT?

INT. MALL - DAY

Teen boys or girls.

          CHARACTER 1
Can I borrow your credit card?

          CHARACTER 2
What for?

          CHARACTER 1
I don't have any cash today - but I will on Friday. So I could pay you back on Friday.

          CHARACTER 2
Why don't you use your card?

          CHARACTER 1
They took it away.

          CHARACTER 2
When?

          CHARACTER 1
Two weeks ago.

          CHARACTER 2
I saw your card in your wallet yesterday.

          CHARACTER 1
That's an old expired card.

          CHARACTER 2
Why are you carrying around an old expired card?

          CHARACTER 1
An expired card is better than no card at all. It's embarrassing to not have a card.

          CHARACTER 2
That's messed up.

          CHARACTER 1
Easy for you to say. You have an American Express card with no limit.

CHARACTER 2
My card is for emergencies only -
or if my parents tell me I can use
it to buy something.

CHARACTER 1
I can't function without a card. I
need stuff.

CHARACTER 2
If I remember correctly, you needed
too much stuff. You were out of
control.

CHARACTER 1
Maybe, but I've learned my lesson.
I deserve a second chance. Don't
you think I deserve a second
chance?

CHARACTER 2
I guess.

CHARACTER 1
Then you'll let me use your card?

CHARACTER 2
No.

CHARACTER 1
Why not?

CHARACTER 2
I don't understand what my American
Express card has to do with your
second chance.

CHARACTER 1
Because if I can prove that I'm
responsible with your card, I can
prove to my parents that I deserve
that second chance.

CHARACTER 2
Ain't gonna happen.

YOUR THERAPY ISN'T WORKING

INT. SCHOOL CAFETERIA - DAY

Teen boys or girls.

          CHARACTER 1
Do my eyes look milky?

          CHARACTER 2
Whaddaya mean?

          CHARACTER 1
My eyes look milky. Check them out. They don't look normal.

          CHARACTER 2
They look the same as always to me.

          CHARACTER 1
No they don't! They are normally shiny and bright. And now they aren't.

          CHARACTER 2
You're freaking out!

          CHARACTER 1
I'm not! There's something seriously wrong with me. I think it's my gall bladder or my tryoid.

          CHARACTER 2
It's "thyroid" not "tryoid."

          CHARACTER 1
What difference does it make if I'm dying?

          CHARACTER 2
Did you ever think about seeing a psychiatrist?

          CHARACTER 1
I do. Every Tuesday and Thursday 4:00-5:00.

          CHARACTER 2
You should quit.

          CHARACTER 1
Why? I've been going for years.

                    CHARACTER 2
              Because it isn't working!

SCENES FOR KIDS OR TEENS - DRAMATIC

STANDING UP TO THE BULLY

INT. SCHOOL CAFETERIA - DAY

Kids or Teens.

                BULLY
Hey newbie, wanna join our club?

                NEW KID
Really?

                BULLY
Yeah sure. You just have to agree to a dare and eat this first.

                NEW KID
No way. I'm not eating that!

                BULLY
Come on. It looks good.

                NEW KID
You're crazy. It looks disgusting!

                BULLY
If you want in, you have to eat it.

The new kid thinks about it.

                NEW KID
Ok, ok.

                BULLY
            (handing it over)
Here. Hurry up.

                NEW KID
Alright, give me a second!

The new kid tries to eat it, but can't.

                NEW KID (CONT'D)
Yuck!!! I just can't...

                BULLY
I knew you wouldn't do it. You're just a chicken.

                NEW KID
I am not!

> BULLY
> You are too!

> NEW KID
> Whatever.

> BULLY
> This just proves that you aren't cool enough to be in our club.

> NEW KID
> Fine. I don't want to be in your stupid club anyway.

> BULLY
> You calling us stupid!?!?

> NEW KID
> I didn't call *you* stupid. I called the *club* stupid.

> BULLY
> You better watch your step from now on.

> NEW KID
> Oooh, I'm so scared.

RUN!

EXT. TOUGH NEIGHBORHOOD - NIGHT

Kids or Teens.

                CHARACTER 1
We have to go! I mean now!

                CHARACTER 2
What? What's the big rush?

                CHARACTER 1
Those creepy guys are coming.

                CHARACTER 2
Where?

                CHARACTER 1
Around the corner.

                CHARACTER 2
Who are they anyway?

                CHARACTER 1
I don't know, but I heard them talking at the convenience store - and it was some bad stuff they were planning.

                CHARACTER 2
Ok. Let's go to the police. That's the smart thing to do.

                CHARACTER 1
I think one of them is the police.

                CHARACTER 2
That's not good.

                CHARACTER 1
Can we go now?

                CHARACTER 2
Heck yes.

SCENES FOR KIDS OR TEENS – DRAMATIC/COMEDIC

STUDENT SHRINK

INT. CLASSROOM - DAY

Kid or teen with adult.

Try this scene as both dramatic and comedic.

          STACEY
Excuse me Mr. Thomas. May I speak with you for a minute?

          MR. T
Is it really important?

          STACEY
Yes, it is.

          MR. T
Well, I really need to be running. You'll have to make it quick.

          STACEY
I'm sorry I have to tell you this, but your attitude around here lately really has been bumming all of us kids out and I'd just like to know why you've been so grumpy and uninterested in what your students are doing these days. Is it something we did?

          MR. T
I don't know what you're talking about.

          STACEY
I'm sorry but you just act weird all the time.

          MR. T
Stacey...you are one of the brightest kids I've ever had in my classes, but that doesn't mean that you are allowed to criticize me as your teacher.

          STACEY
Well, if I don't say anything no one else will.

MR. T
First of all I think you are mistaken and that I am acting no differently now than I ever have...not that I need to explain myself to one of my students. End of discussion.

STACEY
You know Mr. Thomas...this is my education and I think I have the right to say something if I'm being bummed out by my favorite teacher...in my favorite class.

MR. T
Ok...what exactly do you not like that I'm doing? You do understand that class can't always be fun.

STACEY
I'm sorry but class is never fun. You never smile and no one in the class ever smiles. It's a real drag.

MR. T
Well, excuse me for being such a downer but I do have other things on my mind besides what goes on here.

STACEY
You want to talk about it?

MR. T
What?

STACEY
I said...do you want to talk about it?

MR. T
Talk about what?

STACEY
The problems you're having at home.

MR. T
Who said that I'm having problems at home?

STACEY
You are, aren't you?

MR. T
I can't believe that I'm being analyzed by one of my students.

STACEY
Well, somebody has to do it. Have you seen a shrink yet?

MR. T
No.

STACEY
Why not?

MR. T
Because it's not that bad.

STACEY
What?

MR. T
What's bothering me.

STACEY
So there is something bothering you?

MR. T
I never said that and I would appreciate it if you would stay out of my personal life.

STACEY
Somehow I knew you would say that. If you decide you want to talk about it...let me know.

COUNTY FAIR CRISIS

EXT. COUNTY FAIR - DAY

Kids or teens, boys or girls.

          CHARACTER 1
Let's ride the Octopus!

          CHARACTER 2
How about we do the Ferris wheel again?

          CHARACTER 1
We did it three times already.

          CHARACTER 2
But you have the best view from the Ferris wheel.

          CHARACTER 1
Are you afraid of the Octopus?

          CHARACTER 2
No! I am not afraid of anything.

          CHARACTER 1
You won't ride on the Octopus - you won't do FreeFall, the Tilt-A-Whirl, Skydiver, or Fireball.

          CHARACTER 2
That doesn't mean I'm afraid.

          CHARACTER 1
What does it mean? You will only do the Carousel, Teacups, and the other "Kiddie Rides."

          CHARACTER 2
OK! OK! I'm not afraid. I get sick and puke.

          CHARACTER 1
How do you know?

          CHARACTER 2
Because I've tried to ride the cool rides - and every time - I've puked. Are you happy now?

CHARACTER 1
Why didn't you tell me that at the beginning?

CHARACTER 2
I was too embarrassed.

CHARACTER 1
We're friends. You can tell me anything. Let's go look at the baby pigs.

CHARACTER 2
Good idea.

FISH TANK TERROR

Kids or teens, boys or girls.

Actor Note – use your imagination. Try as a drama or comedy.

CHARACTER 1
Ok, I'm going to show you something, but you have to promise not to scream.

CHARACTER 2
Why would I scream?

CHARACTER 1
You'll see. Do you promise?

CHARACTER 2
I promise. But I am not a screamer.

CHARACTER 1
Oh, really?

CHARACTER 2
Ok, maybe that one time at the fair. But that stupid clown was creepy – and he jumped out at me.

CHARACTER 1
What I'm about to show you cannot be mentioned to anyone. Not Jack – not Missy – not your brother. Nobody.

CHARACTER 2
Why?

CHARACTER 1
Because I said so. And they might panic.

CHARACTER 2
This better be really something special the way you're building it up.

CHARACTER 1
You'll see.

CHARACTER 2
Where is it?

                    CHARACTER 1
          Under this box. I have "it" trapped
          in my old fish tank.

                    CHARACTER 2
          What is "it"?

Character 1 pulls the box off the fish tank.

                    CHARACTER 1
          This!

                    CHARACTER 2
          What the heck is that?

                    CHARACTER 1
          You tell me.

SUGAR ISN'T YOUR FRIEND

EXT. NEIGHBORHOOD – DAY

Kids or teens, boys or girls.

Two friends are walking home from school.

          CHARACTER 1
Wanna grab a candy bar at my house?

          CHARACTER 2
I can't.

          CHARACTER 1
Why not?

          CHARACTER 2
My mom says they're terrible for me.

          CHARACTER 1
Wrong! They are good for quick energy.

          CHARACTER 2
Too much sugar.

          CHARACTER 1
Too much sugar? What about a Snickers bar? That's just peanuts and good stuff.

          CHARACTER 2
Mom says the "good stuff" is the "bad stuff" – and the peanuts have mold.

          CHARACTER 1
What about Skittles?

          CHARACTER 2
Is your mom trying to kill you?

          CHARACTER 1
What do you mean?

          CHARACTER 2
Skittles are the worst.

CHARACTER 1
What are you talking about? Even my
dad loves Skittles.

CHARACTER 2
How much does your dad weigh?

CHARACTER 1
I guess I see your point.

TIME MACHINE

INT. SCIENCE LABORATORY - DAY

Kids or teens, boys.

Billy and Jess are in Jess's father's science laboratory. They are standing behind the time machine that Jess's father has built.

                BILLY
What if we get stuck in some kind of dinosaur age or something?

                JESS
We won't.

                BILLY
But how do you know?

                JESS
Because my dad is a genius.

                BILLY
A lot of people think he is a little nutty. I don't - but some people do.

                JESS
My dad is just way ahead of everyone else. His time machine is ready to go. I heard him say so.

                BILLY
I wanna go to the future then. I wanna see what it's like.

                JESS
We can't go into the future. We would be like the dumbest people on the planet. We would be like our grandparents are now. They don't know anything about texting or video games. We would be so far behind we would never catch up.

                BILLY
Then where are we going?

                    JESS
We're going back before my mother
died. I want to know her - and talk
to her. All I know about her is
from old pictures and stories my
dad has told me.

                    BILLY
Your dad is really gonna get mad
when he finds out you used his time
machine before he did.

                    JESS
We.

                    BILLY
I didn't say I was going.

                    JESS
You have to go. We're blood
brothers.

                    BILLY
Oh, right.

WHAT'S IN YOUR HAND?

INT. FAST FOOD RESTAURANT - DAY

Kids or teens, boys or girls.

Character 1 comes in late. Character 2 quickly hides a present behind her/his back.

          CHARACTER 1
What's that?

          CHARACTER 2
Nothin'.

          CHARACTER 1
You had something in your hand. What is it?

          CHARACTER 2
I don't have anything in my hand.

          CHARACTER 1
I saw you with something in your hand...and then you put it behind your back.

          CHARACTER 2
I'm not going to show it to you.

          CHARACTER 1
Why not?

          CHARACTER 2
I can't tell you.

          CHARACTER 1
Is it something you took from me?

          CHARACTER 2
No.

          CHARACTER 1
Yes it is. It must be or you would let me see it.

          CHARACTER 2
I can't show you. If I do, it will ruin everything.

CHARACTER 1
What do you mean it will ruin everything?

CHARACTER 2
Gosh...why can't you just let it go? You'll know soon enough.

CHARACTER 1
What do you mean by that?

CHARACTER 2
I said too much already, so just stop asking questions.

CHARACTER 1
It's something for me, isn't it?

CHARACTER 2
Forget it. Just take it. Yes, it's for you. I hope you're happy.

CHARACTER 1
I just wanted to know what was in your hand.

SCENES FOR KIDS OR TEENS - COMEDIC

FAVORITE SNEAKERS

INT. SCHOOL - DAY

Kids or teens.

          CHARACTER 1
Can I ask you a question about your Nikes?

          CHARACTER 2
Sure.

          CHARACTER 1
How long have you had them?

          CHARACTER 2
A long time.

          CHARACTER 1
Too long, I'd say.

          CHARACTER 2
What are you talking about?

          CHARACTER 1
They are totally worn out - and sometimes I swear I can smell them.

          CHARACTER 2
I love these Nikes!

          CHARACTER 1
Why?

          CHARACTER 2
They've been good to me.

          CHARACTER 1
I have no idea what that even means, but you are way cooler than your Nikes.

          CHARACTER 2
Maybe next year.

          CHARACTER 1
They don't even look like they fit anymore. You might end up with Clubfoot or something.

                    CHARACTER 2
Really?

                    CHARACTER 1
Do you really want to take a
chance?

                    CHARACTER 2
I guess not. I have a new pair in
my closet.

                    CHARACTER 1
How long have you had the new pair?

                    CHARACTER 2
Two years.

                    CHARACTER 1
There is something wrong with your
brain.

TINY HOUSE

EXT. HOUSE - DAY

Kids or teens.

CHARACTER 1 is standing in his/her front yard selling what appears to be everything he/she owns. A neighborhood friend comes by the house to see what's going on.

                    CHARACTER 1
Wanna buy some great stuff?

                    CHARACTER 2
Why do you have all your stuff on your lawn?

                    CHARACTER 1
I'm selling almost everything.

                    CHARACTER 2
Why?

                    CHARACTER 1
Because my parents want to buy a "Tiny House" and they say I can only bring my absolute favorite clothes and stuff.

                    CHARACTER 2
That's weird. I've seen the TV show. They are really tiny.

                    CHARACTER 1
Tell me about it.

                    CHARACTER 2
Are you guys broke?

                    CHARACTER 1
No. They just want to live a stress-free life they say. Vacation more and travel a lot.

                    CHARACTER 2
That sounds pretty good.

                    CHARACTER 1
I guess.

CHARACTER 2
Where are you going to put the Tiny House?

CHARACTER 1
My grandparents have a huge back yard.

CHARACTER 2
Gotcha. That's a lot of cool stuff you're getting rid of.

CHARACTER 1
I know.

CHARACTER 2
I want it all. How much? Our house is huge.

WEIRD COUSIN FRANK

EXT. SCHOOL DROP OFF ZONE - DAY

Kids or Teens.

          CHARACTER 1

Hi.

          CHARACTER 2

Who's that weird guy who just dropped you off?

          CHARACTER 1

That weird guy is my cousin Frank.

          CHARACTER 2

Why's he dropping you off instead of your mom?

          CHARACTER 1

He's staying with us for a while and he has to earn his keep.

          CHARACTER 2

What's that mean?

          CHARACTER 1

I guess that means he doesn't get to eat for free like me.

          CHARACTER 2

How old is he?

          CHARACTER 1

I think he's like 17 maybe.

          CHARACTER 2

Why's he staying with you guys?

          CHARACTER 1

Because my aunt kicked him out.

          CHARACTER 2

Why did she kick him out?

          CHARACTER 1

Because he got a stupid haircut and a stupid tattoo.

                    CHARACTER 2
          There's a lot of stupid haircuts
          and stupid tattoos around these
          days.

                    CHARACTER 1
          Tell me about it.

                    CHARACTER 2
          I'm never gonna have a stupid
          haircut...or a stupid tattoo.

                    CHARACTER 1
          Me neither.

DOG TREATS AREN'T FOR HUMANS

INT. LIBRARY - DAY

Kids or teens.

          CHARACTER 1
Wow! What happened to your face?

          CHARACTER 2
Don't scream it out for the whole world to hear.

          CHARACTER 1
I'm sorry - but it's not like you can keep it a secret. What is that?

          CHARACTER 2
My doctor says it's an allergic reaction.

          CHARACTER 1
It looks horrible!

          CHARACTER 2
Hey, don't make me feel any worse than I already do.

          CHARACTER 1
So what are you allergic to?

          CHARACTER 2
I don't wanna say.

          CHARACTER 1
Why not?

          CHARACTER 2
I just don't.

          CHARACTER 1
Was it something you ate?

          CHARACTER 2
I don't want to talk about it.

          CHARACTER 1
I have a cousin that would break out if a cat licked him.

          CHARACTER 2
That's not it.

CHARACTER 1
I would tell you if it happened to me.

CHARACTER 2
Ok. I ate some dog treats.

CHARACTER 1
Why would you do that?

CHARACTER 2
I love the way they smell - and Axel loves them - so I just thought I would try one. They were really good so I ate a few more. I couldn't stop myself. They're really good.

CHARACTER 1
I wish you hadn't told me now. You just totally grossed me out.

GOIN' VEGETARIAN

INT. SCHOOL LUNCHROOM - DAY

Two kids or teens in a school lunchroom.

          CHARACTER 1
What is that stuff?

          CHARACTER 2
That is hummus.

          CHARACTER 1
What is hummus?

          CHARACTER 2
Mom says it's really healthy.

          CHARACTER 1
What's it taste like?

          CHARACTER 2
I don't know - I throw it away.

          CHARACTER 1
Maybe it's really good.

          CHARACTER 2
I don't care. I am rebelling. Mom decided to change everything because she says we need to eat healthier. I liked things the way they were.

          CHARACTER 1
Can I try that "home us" stuff?

          CHARACTER 2
It's not "home us." It's "hum mus." Take it. I'm not eating it. And I'm not eating these carrots and celery either.

          CHARACTER 1
This stuff is pretty good. Wanna trade?

          CHARACTER 2
Whatcha got?

          CHARACTER 1
Lunchables.

                        CHARACTER 2
                  Now you're talkin'.

I HATE MATH

INT. LIBRARY - DAY

Kids or teens.

CHARACTER 1
I hate math!!

CHARACTER 2
How can you hate it? You're getting an A in math.

CHARACTER 1
Just because you're good at something doesn't mean you like it.

CHARACTER 2
I like math - but I'm getting a C.

CHARACTER 1
I like soccer but I'm the worst on my team.

CHARACTER 2
And I don't even like soccer - but I'm the best on my team.

CHARACTER 1
Why do you play then?

CHARACTER 2
My dad says I need the exercise.

CHARACTER 1
The world is weird.

CHARACTER 2
Sometimes things just don't make sense.

CHARACTER 1
Wish we could switch talents.

CHARACTER 2
Me too.

MOTORCYCLES NEED KEYS

LOCATION - ACTOR'S CHOICE

Kids or Teens.

>   ASHTON
> My sister has a new boyfriend.
>
>   PARKER
> I saw him with her.
>
>   ASHTON
> He rides a motorcycle.
>
>   PARKER
> I thought your parents said you and your sister were never allowed on a motorcycle.
>
>   ASHTON
> They didn't exactly say that. They said we couldn't "ride" on a motorcycle.
>
>   PARKER
> I don't understand.
>
>   ASHTON
> She doesn't "ride" on the motorcycle...she just "sits" on the seat and puts her arms around his waist.
>
>   PARKER
> That's kinda goofy.
>
>   ASHTON
> They do that for hours.
>
>   PARKER
> Why?
>
>   ASHTON
> I guess they think it's cool and romantic.
>
>   PARKER
> Where is she now?

ASHTON
Parked on Main Street...sitting on the back of that motorcycle with her boyfriend...looking all dangerous.

PARKER
How do you know that?

ASHTON
Because mom and I dropped her off downtown an hour ago---and we're picking her up in two hours.

PARKER
How do you know she won't ride around with him after you left?

ASHTON
Because mom made him give her the keys to the motorcycle until we get my sister back.

PARKER
Good thinking.

DON'T FEED THIS DOG

EXT. NEIGHBORHOOD - DAY

Kids or teens.

                    CHARACTER 1
My dog is sick.

                    CHARACTER 2
What's wrong with him?

                    CHARACTER 1
I think it's something he ate.

                    CHARACTER 2
What did he eat?

                    CHARACTER 1
Everything.

                    CHARACTER 2
What do you mean?

                    CHARACTER 1
He has a problem with food. He's a pig. He has no control.

                    CHARACTER 2
Why don't you stop giving him so much to eat?

                    CHARACTER 1
He begs for it. It's so hard to resist him when he looks at you with those sad eyes.

                    CHARACTER 2
I know. He comes to our house and begs too. We can't resist him either.

                    CHARACTER 1
And then he goes to the Murphy's house and begs them.

                    CHARACTER 2
The vet says he needs to lose 15 pounds or he could die.

CHARACTER 1
I'm going to make a flyer and put it up all over the neighborhood that says "DON'T FEED THIS DOG."

CHARACTER 2
That might work.

CHARACTER 1
And if that doesn't work - he's grounded and confined to our house.

CHARACTER 2
But then he won't get any exercise.

CHARACTER 1
Mom says we can put him on the treadmill.

HAPPY MOM?

INT. BEDROOM - NIGHT

Kids or teens, boys or girls.

Sister or brother comes into sister's (or brother's) bedroom and shuts the door.

              CHARACTER 1
Notice anything different with mom?

              CHARACTER 2
No.

              CHARACTER 1
Well - she's acting weird.

              CHARACTER 2
How?

              CHARACTER 1
She's smiling all the time.

              CHARACTER 2
Is that bad?

              CHARACTER 1
Never happened before.

              CHARACTER 2
Maybe she's happy.

              CHARACTER 1
But why all of a sudden?

              CHARACTER 2
I don't know.

              CHARACTER 1
Go ask her.

              CHARACTER 2
You go ask her.

              CHARACTER 1
I'm not asking her.

              CHARACTER 2
Why not?

                    CHARACTER 1
          It's probably a good thing - and I
          don't want to mess it up.

                    CHARACTER 2
          Good idea.

                    CHARACTER 1
          Might be a good time to ask her for
          a new phone.

                    CHARACTER 2
          I want a new phone too.

                    CHARACTER 1
          Let's go ask her. Smile.

BIG DAY AT THE BUFFET

Kids or teens, boys or girls.

Pick your favorite location.

          CHARACTER 1
I don't feel so good.

          CHARACTER 2
Where?

          CHARACTER 1
My stomach.

          CHARACTER 2
No wonder.

          CHARACTER 1
What do you mean?

          CHARACTER 2
You ate too much.

          CHARACTER 1
It was a buffet.

          CHARACTER 2
That doesn't mean you have to eat some of everything - and then go back for seconds.

          CHARACTER 1
I couldn't help it. It was so good.

          CHARACTER 2
But you're sick now.

          CHARACTER 1
I'll get over it. Got any TUMS?

          CHARACTER 2
What's TUMS?

          CHARACTER 1
That's what you take after you eat at a buffet.

          CHARACTER 2
You are a sick person.

CHARACTER 1
But I won't be hungry for a couple of days.

CHARACTER 2
You're not a bear getting ready for winter.

CHARACTER 1
Gotta get it while the gettin' is good. That's my motto.

CHARACTER 2
Your motto is going to make you fat.

CHARACTER 1
Fat and happy.

GOTTA GET RICH

Kids or teens, two boys.

Pick your favorite location.

          FRANKIE
I am tired of not having any money. How about you?

          ROSS
Tell me about it. I am always begging for money - and I hate it.

          FRANKIE
My mom is like Fort Knox. She doesn't want to let go of a penny.

          ROSS
I've resorted to borrowing from my sister - but she charges me 10% a day.

          FRANKIE
That is wrong!

          ROSS
Something has to change. I can't wait until I am out of college to be rich.

          FRANKIE
We need it now!

          ROSS
Absolutely!

          FRANKIE
Got any ideas?

          ROSS
Let me think.

          FRANKIE
Food things are always good.

          ROSS
Yeah - people will eat anything.

          FRANKIE
John Milken eats dog biscuits. I know we can make something better than that.

ROSS
My mom paid $18 a pound for fish - and fish is gross. We can surely come up with something that isn't gross.

FRANKIE
I hear they eat cats in Asia.

ROSS
Are you suggesting we feed people cat? Because I am not feeding people cat.

FRANKIE
I was just making a point - about how people will eat anything if you tell them it's good.

ROSS
Kool Aid. How hard was that to come up with - and people have been drinking it since caveman times.

FRANKIE
You're starting to make me hungry.

ROSS
Me too. Let's get a snack and think about it.

FRANKIE
Great idea, Ross.

SILVER LININGS

INT. HOSPITAL - DAY

Kids or teens, boys or girls.

              CHARACTER 1
Why me? Why do I have to break my leg?

              CHARACTER 2
Sorry. We're gonna miss you in the rest of the tournament.

              CHARACTER 1
Nothing's going right for me this year. My dog died and now this.

              CHARACTER 2
I guess it could've been a lot worse.

              CHARACTER 1
How do you figure?

              CHARACTER 2
You could've broken both legs...and I could've died.

              CHARACTER 1
That made me feel better for about two seconds.

              CHARACTER 2
Just sayin'.

              CHARACTER 1
We're supposed to go to Disney World in two weeks. I can't walk around all day with crutches. My arms will fall off.

              CHARACTER 2
But maybe you can ride around in a shiny new wheelchair the whole time.

              CHARACTER 1
Maybe.

> CHARACTER 2
I find it exhausting to walk around Disney World all day. You could be pushed around all day long and never get tired.

> CHARACTER 1
Now that just made me feel better.

HERE, KITTY KITTY

Kids or teens, boys or girls.

There's a third character in this scene...the cat!

Make sure you actually "see" the cat. Look for it in the beginning and see it when it comes up. Visualize.

          CHARACTER 1
Here kitty kitty...here kitty kitty.

          CHARACTER 2
That cat doesn't like people.

          CHARACTER 1
All cats love me. I'm a cat person. Here kitty kitty.

          CHARACTER 2
I'm warning you, he'll bite you or something.

          CHARACTER 1
Don't be silly.

          CHARACTER 2
Last week he took off my little brother's pinky.

          CHARACTER 1
Really?

          CHARACTER 2
Yeah...it was cool.

          CHARACTER 1
That's gross! Oh look, here he comes right over to me. I told you cats like me.

          CHARACTER 2
That's weird. He usually hates people.

          CHARACTER 1
Hi there. Oh you're so soft...Ouch! He bit me!

SCENES FOR KIDS - DRAMATIC/COMEDIC

DOGS HATE ME

INT. SCHOOL - DAY

Two friends (kids).

                    CHARACTER 1
Great news!

                    CHARACTER 2
What?

                    CHARACTER 1
Mom says you can come stay at our house for the whole weekend.

                    CHARACTER 2
   (worried)
I think my mom will be ok with that.

                    CHARACTER 1
The weather is supposed to be great so we can hang out by the pool all weekend.

                    CHARACTER 2
Got a question for you.

                    CHARACTER 1
What?

                    CHARACTER 2
Do you have any pets?

                    CHARACTER 1
Yes. Why?

                    CHARACTER 2
What do you have?

                    CHARACTER 1
Two cats, 20 fish, and a dog.

                    CHARACTER 2
That's what I was afraid of.

                    CHARACTER 1
What do you mean?

                    CHARACTER 2
Dogs hate me.

         CHARACTER 1
That's silly.

         CHARACTER 2
No, really. They hate me.

         CHARACTER 1
Dogs hate you?

         CHARACTER 2
Absolutely. I have been bitten at least 20 times in my life.

         CHARACTER 1
What did you do to them?

         CHARACTER 2
Nothing. I don't even have to look at them.

         CHARACTER 1
And then they just bite you?

         CHARACTER 2
Yep.

         CHARACTER 1
Maybe it's all in your mind.

         CHARACTER 2
I have scars all over my body.

         CHARACTER 1
Show me.

         CHARACTER 2
    (showing scars)
This was from a Dachshund. This was from a German Shepherd. Here's one from a Beagle. Chihuahua. Pug. Yorkie.

         CHARACTER 1
    (amazed at all the scars)
Wow! Dogs do hate you.

NO CATS

EXT. HOUSE – DAY

Kids, boys or girls.

Character 1 & 2 are sitting on the porch of Character 2's home. Character 2's cat is sitting on the lap of character 2.

     CHARACTER 1
Your cat is so cool.

     CHARACTER 2
I know.

     CHARACTER 1
What's her name?

     CHARACTER 2
Magic.

     CHARACTER 1
Why did you name her Magic?

     CHARACTER 2
Because one day I wished for a cat. The next day she was here – like magic.

     CHARACTER 1
She just appeared?

     CHARACTER 2
Yep.

     CHARACTER 1
Your Mom and Dad didn't just buy her?

     CHARACTER 2
Nope. They swear they didn't.

     CHARACTER 1
That's pretty hard to believe.

     CHARACTER 2
I know. That's why it had to be magic.

CHARACTER 1
I always wanted a cat.

CHARACTER 2
Why don't you wish for one - like I did?

CHARACTER 1
First, I have to wish that my Dad isn't allergic to cats.

CHARACTER 2
Your Dad is allergic to cats?

CHARACTER 1
Yes. So we can't have a cat.

CHARACTER 2
Maybe you should wish for a dog.

ALAN DYSERT

Millions of people in the United States and around the world know Alan as Sean Cudahy from the ABC soap opera *All My Children*. Alan's five-year portrayal (over 500 episodes) of the devious, yet humorous cad landed him on the cover of national magazines, including *People*, and made him a regular guest on such shows as *Regis and Kathie Lee*, *Sally Jessy Raphael*, *The Merv Griffin Show*, and as a co-host of *The Mike Douglas Show*.

Alan has also been seen nationwide on prime-time television, in films, and in national commercials. His commercial credits include *Toyota*, *Chrysler*, *Atari*, *Lee Jeans*, and others.

He has served as an executive producer on six feature films and recently completed filming a comedy film he wrote, directed, produced, and starred in called *The Senator*.

Alan has taught the craft of acting and personal communication skills to more than 4,000 people over the past 25 years - more than any coach east of the Mississippi. He has taken his special style of teaching actors to Nashville, Chicago, Memphis, Miami, Orlando, Atlanta, and many other cities.

His acting and music clients include major TV and music stars. Alan's clients hold nine Grammys, 15 CMA Awards, a Golden Globe nomination, and an MTV Video Music Award for Video of the Year.

Alan earned his Bachelor of Science degree from the College of Communications (TV, Film, and Radio) at the University of Illinois, where he was a James Scholar, a member of The Honor Society of Phi Kappa Phi, and graduated with High Honors.

The Actor's School (ActorsSchoolUSA.com), which Alan founded, is the largest training center for actors, singers, voice-over artists, and public speakers in the South.

Made in the USA
Las Vegas, NV
31 December 2023